The V.I.S.I.O.N.A.R.Y Blueprint for Kingdom Entrepreneurs

YOUR 90-DAY STRATEGY TO TRANSFORM VISION, UNLOCK POTENTIAL, AND MULTIPLY WEALTH

DR. ARLEEN A. FULLER, PH.D.

SERIAL ENTREPRENUER
10X BUSINESS COACH LICENSEE

TABLE OF CONTENTS

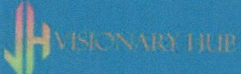

Dedication Page

This work was created by Dr. Arleen A. Fuller, a Certified 10X Business Coach Licensee under Grant Cardone. As a teenager with ten streams of income, I discovered my purpose in starting and scaling businesses while empowering others to do the same.

I dedicate this work to my beloved parents, **Lawrence Fuller Jr.** and **Daveola Jackson Fuller**, whose lives exemplified ambition, discipline, integrity, morality, humanitarianism, and an entrepreneurial spirit. It was through their example that I first grasped the concept of the *"Power to Create Wealth."* From an early age, my parents instilled in me the importance of **Self-Actualization**—the ability to reach our full potential.

Their unwavering commitment to serving others inspires my work today. All scripture referenced within these pages is sourced from the Holy Bible (*KJV, NIV, MSG*), the foundation of my faith and guiding principles.

— **Dr. Arleen A. Fuller**

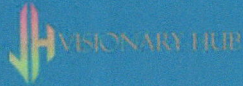

About the Author

My name is Dr. Arleen A. Fuller, and I am known as the original Serial Entrepreneur, long before the term became popular. At 64 years old, I look back on a lifetime of entrepreneurial experience rooted in hard work, service, and faith.

From the age of 14 to 19, I managed at least ten streams of income. Although I held great jobs, I prioritized working for myself, embodying the spirit of entrepreneurship I learned from my parents. About 95% of my income went toward helping those in need—a value demonstrated by my parents in their everyday lives.

Some of my early income streams included:

- Working at a senior citizen center teaching arts and crafts
- Typing over 100 words per minute
- Accountant/bookkeeping services
- Singer/songwriter/musician
- Political canvasser
- Income tax preparer
- Shift manager at Burger King
- Licensed Master Cosmetologist/Master Hair Braider
- Office assistant (filing, answering phones)
- Biblical studies instructor

My father, a Seer and Prophet, stressed the importance of reading and self-reliance. I absorbed encyclopedias, business books, and anything that would expand my knowledge.

Introduction: The Power of 90 Days

Purpose:

This workbook is designed to help you achieve extraordinary results by breaking your goals into manageable, strategic steps over 90 days.

Scriptural Foundation:

- *"Write the vision, and make it plain upon tables, that he may run that readeth it."* — Habakkuk 2:2

- *"For it is he that giveth thee power to get wealth."* — Deuteronomy 8:18

The V.I.S.I.O.N.A.R.Y Framework

This workbook is structured around the nine pillars of the V.I.S.I.O.N.A.R.Y system:

- *Vision-Driven, Imaginative, Strategic Mindset, Innovative, Originator, Nonconventional, Ambitious, Risk Taker, Yielded to the Process.*

About This Workbook

This 90-day guide combines biblical principles with practical strategies to help you:

1. Apply the V.I.S.I.O.N.A.R.Y framework using biblical and prophetic principles.

2. How to discern and steward God-given visions and opportunities.

3. How to develop multiple streams of income rooted in biblical principles.

4. How to cultivate integrity, adaptability, and resilience.

5. Yield to spiritual and financial growth through prophetic development.

6. Write and clarify your vision.

7. Implement a strategic business plan.

8. Discover your life's purpose.

Disclaimer: This resource is grounded in *Kingdom Biblical principles* for *Kingdom Entrepreneurs*. All principles herein are derived from the Bible. If biblical principles trigger you, then this workbook may not be a good fit.

My Legacy of Inspiration

- **My father** was a pastor, paint contractor, television and radio repairman, and the owner of a BBQ restaurant—where more than half the food was donated to those in need.

- **My mother** was a Master Cosmetologist, Cosmetology Instructor, clothing designer, Biblical Teacher, and nail technician.

Both were humanitarians and philanthropists, modeling selfless dedication that shaped my life's purpose. As you move through this workbook, my hope is that you, too, will discover your calling, embrace your vision, and take bold steps toward achieving it.

How to Use This Workbook

1. **Set Aside Time Daily:** Commit to at least 15–30 minutes each day to fill out the planner, reflect, and pray.

2. **Review Your Goals Weekly:** Use the weekly reflection to evaluate progress, challenges, and triumphs.

3. **Engage with the V.I.S.I.O.N.A.R.Y Framework:** Each framework is accompanied by scripture, reflection prompts, and action steps.

4. **Stay Open and Yielded:** Trust God's guidance throughout this 90-day journey, and expect transformation as you remain obedient to the process.

Foreword: The Spiritual Foundation of The V.I.S.I.O.N.A.R.Y Blueprint

I, **Dr. Arleen A. Fuller,** created this 90-Day Workbook because I saw a dire need in our churches, businesses, and communities for a biblically grounded, practical guide to financial empowerment. Far too often, I've witnessed small congregations struggling to cover their expenses, pastors feeling pressured to lean on members with limited means, and entrepreneurs barely staying afloat. Yet, I believe with all my heart that *each of us is born with every gift we need to thrive and create wealth for our families* — gifts that come directly from God.

In this workbook, I want to show you how to tap into those gifts without placing undue financial burdens on the very people you're called to serve. Below are the key scriptures that form the foundation of **The V.I.S.I.O.N.A.R.Y Hub** model. They combine faith and action, reminding us that while God blesses and empowers us, we must also steward our talents strategically.

1. Deuteronomy 8:18 (KJV)

"But thou shalt remember the LORD thy God: for it is he that giveth thee power to get wealth, that he may establish his covenant..."

- **Divine Empowerment:** God is the ultimate source of our ability to create wealth. We must operate with gratitude, humility, and dependence on Him.

- **Innovative Ideas & Strategies:** This "power to get wealth" often manifests through our God-given talents, creative solutions, and disciplined hard work.

- **Greater Purpose:** Wealth is not for self-aggrandizement but to establish God's covenant, build His kingdom, and create generational impact.

I've always disliked the notion of burdening those who already struggle financially. **Deuteronomy 8:18** reassures us that everyone has the capacity to contribute meaningfully and sustain themselves—without relying on a few to shoulder all the responsibility.

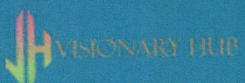

2. Ecclesiastes 11:1–2 (KJV)

"Cast thy bread upon the waters: for thou shalt find it after many days. Give a portion to seven, and also to eight; for thou knowest not what evil shall be upon the earth."

- **Multiple Streams of Income:** King Solomon, renowned for his wisdom, advises having seven or eight sources of revenue. This diversifies risk and ensures stability.

- **Faith in Action:** "Casting your bread upon the waters" symbolizes stepping out in faith, trusting you'll see a return in due time.

- **Practical Preparedness:** Unforeseen challenges arise in life. Having multiple streams of income helps you remain resilient and avoid financial crises.

From a young age, I witnessed how multiple income streams can strengthen a family or community. Ecclesiastes 11:1–2 confirms that God's wisdom includes practical steps for financial security and freedom.

3. Proverbs 29:18 (KJV)

"Where there is no vision, the people perish: but he that keepeth the law, happy is he."

- **Essential Direction:** A lack of vision leads to confusion and eventual failure.
- **Ethical Foundation:** Genuine success involves discipline, integrity, and adherence to Godly principles.
- **Visionary Identity:** The V.I.S.I.O.N.A.R.Y Hub helps participants discover their unique calling and align it with a larger kingdom purpose.

We've all seen ministries, businesses, or families drift aimlessly when no clear vision is in place. Proverbs 29:18 stresses that a God-centered plan is the anchor that keeps us from perishing in uncertainty.

4. Ephesians 3:20 (NIV)

"Now to him who is able to do immeasurably more than all we ask or imagine, according to his power that is at work within us."

- **Boundless Possibilities:** God's power far exceeds our own understanding or perceived limits.

- **Fuel for Ambition:** Faith paves the way for bigger dreams and extraordinary breakthroughs.

- **Divine Power Within:** This verse reminds us that God works through us, enabling outcomes greater than we could ever dream.

Observing people struggle financially is heartbreaking. Ephesians 3:20 encourages us that God not only provides resources but multiplies our efforts beyond our greatest imagination—if we're willing to trust Him.

5. Habakkuk 2:1–4 (KJV)

"I will stand upon my watch... Write the vision, and make it plain... though it tarry, wait for it... the just shall live by his faith."

1. Posture of Readiness (v.1):

"I will stand upon my watch…"
Entrepreneurs and leaders should remain vigilant, focused, and attentive to God's direction.

2. Clarity & Action (v.2):

"I will stand upon my watch…"
Entrepreneurs and leaders should remain vigilant, focused, and attentive to God's direction.

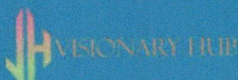

3. Patience & Persistence (v.3):

"…though it tarry, wait for it…"
Delays are part of the journey. Success rarely comes overnight; faith and perseverance bridge the gap.

4. Faith & Humility (v.4):

"…the just shall live by his faith."
Pride and self-reliance can derail us. We must continuously trust God's wisdom, timing, and resources.

This passage from **Habakkuk** encapsulates the heart of The V.I.S.I.O.N.A.R.Y Hub: we adopt a posture of readiness, commit our vision to writing, remain patient amid delays, and walk in faith, confident that God will establish our plans in His perfect time.

Putting It All Together

1. **Deuteronomy 8:18** anchors our conviction that God grants each of us the power to generate wealth for His kingdom purposes.

2. **Ecclesiastes 11:1–2** advises diversifying income streams, highlighting God's practical wisdom for security and growth.

3. **Proverbs 29:18** warns us of the perils of living without a clear, God-centered vision.

4. **Ephesians 3:20** assures us that God can do immeasurably more than we think, fueling our ambition and innovation.

5. **Habakkuk 2:1–4** brings these lessons together with instructions on readiness, clarity, patience, and unwavering faith.

Every gift and talent you need to prosper already resides within you—God placed them there. In these pages, you'll find both the spiritual framework and practical strategies to unearth those gifts, build a solid plan, and create wealth without placing an unfair burden on those who struggle. My hope is that as you work through this 90-Day Workbook, you'll discover a renewed sense of purpose, confidence, and direction—knowing that God has already empowered you to succeed.

May these scriptures and insights light the path ahead, inspiring you to live out your calling as a visionary leader and steward of God's abundant resources.

— Dr. Arleen A. Fuller, PhD
Founder of The V.I.S.I.O.N.A.R.Y Hub, LLC
Certified 10X Business Coach & Master Mental Health Coach

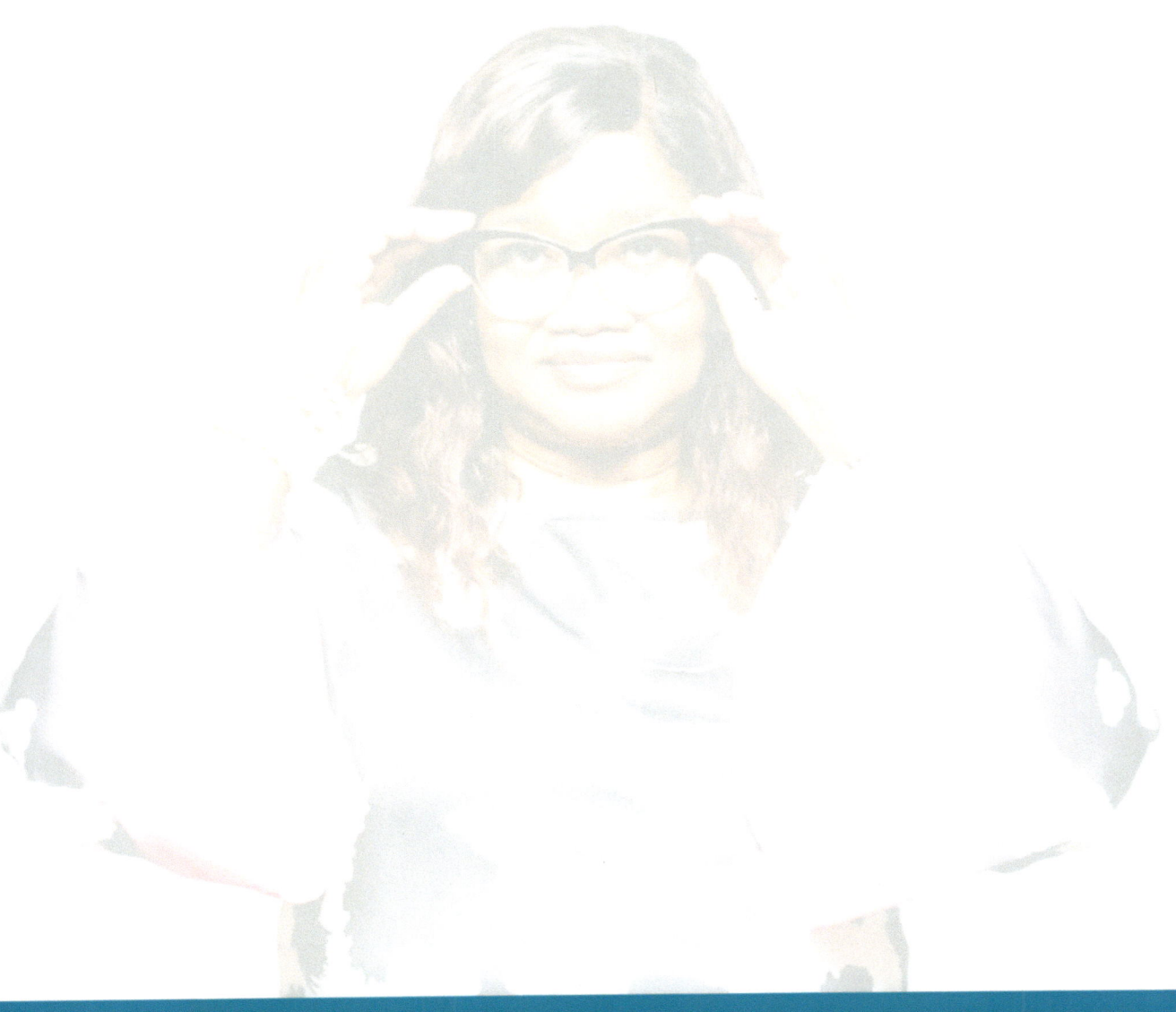

Vision Board Section

Instructions:

- Dedicate 1–2 pages to create your Vision Board.
- Add pictures, words, and symbols that represent your 90-day goals and long-term aspirations.
- Center your board around the theme of your V.I.S.I.O.N.A.R.Y identity (e.g., "Ambitious Risk Taker").
- Reflect on this page daily to stay inspired.

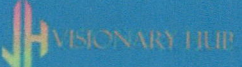

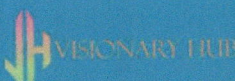

Daily Affirmations and Scriptures

Use these affirmations throughout the 90-day journey to keep your mind and heart aligned with Kingdom principles.

1. I am a visionary leader walking in divine purpose.
2. I am disciplined, strategic, and yielded to the process.
3. I trust God to provide wisdom, resources, and opportunities.
4. I persevere through challenges with faith and resilience.
5. I am an innovator, guided by divine inspiration.
6. I am breaking barriers and creating generational wealth.
7. I attract success, favor, and strategic partnerships.

Faith & Focus Check-In:

- Habakkuk 2:2 – Vision
- Deuteronomy 8:18 – Power to Get Wealth
- Ephesians 3:20 – God Exceeds Our Imagination
- Proverbs 3:5-6 – Trusting in the Lord
- Ecclesiastes 11:1-2 – Diversification & Faith

Notes

The V.I.S.I.O.N.A.R.Y Framework and Scriptures

Vision-Driven
Habakkuk 2:1- 2

Emphasizes the importance of clearly writing and articulating your vision to inspire action and achieve goals.

Nonconventional
Isaiah 43:19

Inspires thinking outside the box, finding solutions in unexpected ways, and embracing God's new paths.

Imaginative
Ephesians 3:20

Encourages bold dreams and reliance on God's power to exceed what we can ask or think.

Ambitious
Philippians 3:13-14

Motivates persistence, striving for excellence, and pursuing the prize of your higher calling.

Strategic Mindset
Luke 14:28-30

Stresses the necessity of planning and preparation before embarking on a venture to ensure success.

Risk-Taker
Matthew 25:14-30

Teaches the value of stewardship and taking calculated risks to multiply the resources entrusted to you.

Innovative
Ecclesiastes 11:1-2

Highlights the importance of diversification, calculated risks, and adaptability to uncertainty.

Yielded To The Process
Proverbs 3:5-6

Encourages trusting in God's guidance and timing, yielding to His will in all entrepreneurial endeavors.

Originator
Genesis 1:26- 28

Calls for creativity and leadership as stewards of God's creation, empowering entrepreneurs to lead boldly.

Each framework is paired with a scripture and action steps to ground you in faith and propel you forward with practical guidance.

VISION-DRIVEN
(Chazon)

Objective: Understanding the importance of prophetic vision and how to clearly define it.

Key Scripture: Habakkuk 2:2 – "Then the LORD replied: 'Write down the revelation and make it plain on tablets so that a herald may run with it.'"

Greek/Hebrew Insight:

Chazon (חָ זוֹן) – Hebrew for "vision" or "revelation." This word implies receiving divine insight and understanding, often through prophetic dreams or visions. In-Depth Study:

What is Prophetic Vision?

A prophetic vision is a divinely inspired revelation, often received through dreams, visions, or spiritual discernment. It involves seeing God's plan for the future and receiving direction for His kingdom purposes.

Reflect on biblical figures such as Joseph (Genesis 37) or Daniel (Daniel 7) who received divine visions and were instructed to steward them.

Receiving and Clarifying Divine Vision:

To receive prophetic vision, it is essential to cultivate a deep relationship with God, positioning yourself in prayer, fasting, and the study of the Word.

- **Reflection Question:** What visions has God already shown you? How clear are they to you?
- **Exercise:** Set aside intentional prayer time to seek clarity on God's vision for your life and calling.

Practical Exercises for Vision Mapping:

After receiving a vision, it's critical to break it down into actionable steps.

- **Activity:** Create a personal vision statement. Write out your short- and long-term goals, ensuring they align with your prophetic calling. Reflection
- **Question:** How does your vision bring glory to God and expand His kingdom?

The Importance of Knowing Your Vision for Personal Life and Its Impact on Entrepreneurship

In the realm of entrepreneurship, having a clear, God-given vision for your personal life is foundational to achieving long-term success. Many people chase after business opportunities or financial ventures without first establishing their personal life vision, and as a result, they often experience burnout, frustration, or lack of direction. Your personal vision acts as a compass, guiding not just your entrepreneurial pursuits but also your purpose in life.

Vision as the Driving Force

A vision is the divine blueprint that reveals your purpose. It's the big picture of what God has called you to do and become. Without vision, you may find yourself walking aimlessly, chasing ideas that don't align with your true calling. Proverbs 29:18 (KJV) says, "Where there is no vision, the people perish." This scripture highlights the vital importance of vision for survival and progress. In entrepreneurship, a lack of vision can cause your ideas to wither, leading to unfulfilled potential and lost opportunities. Your personal vision gives you clarity on why you're building your business and how it fits into God's greater plan for your life.

Vision Provides Focus

Entrepreneurship requires you to make important decisions on a daily basis. When you have a clear vision for your personal life, it becomes easier to filter out distractions and focus on opportunities that align with your values, goals, and divine purpose. Without personal vision, it's easy to become overwhelmed by the countless business ideas or opportunities that may come your way. Vision helps you prioritize your efforts. It sets boundaries around what you say "yes" or "no" to. It keeps you from wasting time on ventures that don't align with your core purpose. Imagine running a business without understanding the "why" behind it—you'd quickly lose motivation, passion, and focus. The same applies to life.

Without Vision, You Can Stifle Growth

Many entrepreneurs fail to grow beyond a certain point, not because they lack skill or talent, but because they lack a solid personal vision. When you don't know where you're going in life, it affects every aspect of your entrepreneurial journey. You may find yourself starting projects and not finishing them, investing in ideas that don't align with your values, or partnering with people whose vision clashes with yours. Entrepreneurial success is rooted in consistency, discipline, and long-term focus—qualities that are only possible when you are clear about your personal vision. If your personal life is chaotic, directionless, or unfocused, this stifles your ability to lead and grow a business successfully. It's impossible to lead a thriving business when you don't have clarity in your own life.

Personal Vision Fuels Entrepreneurial Vision

Your entrepreneurial endeavors should flow from your personal vision. It's important to ask yourself, "What is the legacy I want to leave behind?" "How does this business align with the gifts God has given me?" and "What problem am I called to solve in the marketplace?"

Your personal life vision doesn't just impact your business decisions; it impacts how you lead, how you serve, and how you interact with others. Entrepreneurs who are grounded in a strong sense of personal purpose are able to inspire others, stay resilient during challenges, and build businesses that not only succeed but also make a lasting impact.

Practical Steps for Defining Your Personal Vision

1. **Seek God for Clarity:** Spend time in prayer and the Word to receive God's revelation about your life purpose. Remember, your vision comes from God, not from external pressures or societal expectations.

2. **Write It Down:** Just as God instructed Habakkuk, write the vision down (Habakkuk 2:2). Having a written vision gives you something tangible to refer back to as you make decisions in your personal and professional life.

3. **Align Your Life with Your Vision:** Evaluate how your current actions, relationships, and business ventures align with the vision God has given you. If something doesn't fit, it may be time to make adjustments.

4. **Set Personal Goals:** Once you've clarified your vision, set short-term and long-term goals that align with it. These goals should encompass your personal life, family, spiritual growth, and business endeavors.

5. **Stay Focused on the Big Picture:** There will be distractions and challenges along the way, but staying rooted in your personal vision will keep you focused on your God-given path.

Conclusion

Knowing your personal vision is essential for entrepreneurial success. It creates a solid foundation from which you can build, grow, and sustain a business that is not only financially successful but also aligned with God's greater purpose for your life. Vision keeps you focused, disciplined, and intentional, preventing the confusion and stagnation that can come from wandering without direction. When your personal life and entrepreneurial vision are in sync, you position yourself for supernatural success and lasting impact.

Vision Driven (Chazon)

Reflection:

What do you believe God has called you to accomplish in this season of your life? Write your thoughts below:

....

....

....

Exercise:

Create Your Personal Vision Statement: Write your vision statement based on what you feel God is leading you to do.

....

....

....

....

Mapping Your Goals:

List your short-term and long-term goals that align with your prophetic calling.

Short-term Goals:

....

....

....

....

Long-term Goals:

....

....

....

....

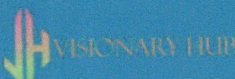

Framework 1: **VISION-DRIVEN**

Scripture

"Write the vision, and make it plain upon tables, that he may run that readeth it." — Habakkuk 2:2 (KJV)

What It Means

A Vision-Driven leader clearly articulates goals, ensuring they are easy to follow and implement. Clarity of vision fosters momentum.

Reflection Prompt

- Write out your vision for your business, ministry, or personal life.

....

....

....

....

....

- Can someone else read it and instantly know how to act on it?

....

....

Action Plan for This Week

1. Refine your vision statement to make it concise and actionable.
2. Share it with a trusted mentor for feedback.
3. Implement any adjustments needed to add clarity.

Part 1: **Clarify Your Vision (Week 1)**

Objective: Define your 90-day goal and align it with your long-term purpose.

Step 1: What Is Your Vision?

Write a clear statement of what you want to achieve in the next 90 days.

- *Example: "I want to generate $50,000 in revenue by launching my new product line."*

....

....

....

....

....

Step 2: Why Does This Matter?

Identify how this goal aligns with your purpose and calling.

- *Example: "This goal supports my mission to create generational wealth and empower others through my business."*

....

....

....

....

Step 3: Visualization Exercise

Imagine yourself achieving this goal. Write a paragraph about how your life will look and feel.

- *Key Question: How does this vision impact your family, business, and legacy?*

....

....

....

....

Daily Planner Template

DATE: /   /

_____

05:00

06:00

07:00

08:00

09:00

10:00

11:00

12:00

13:00

14:00

15:00

16:00

17:00

18:00

19:00

20:00

21:00

22:00

23:00

Top 3 Priorities for the Day

1. ....
2. ....
3. ....

Morning Routine (Set the Tone)

- Scripture/Affirmation of the Day:
- Gratitude List (3 Things):
  1. ....
  2. ....
  3. ....
- Vision Statement: Write down your overarching 90-day vision in one sentence.

....
....
....
....
....

Evening Reflection (Close the Day)

- Biggest Win Today:

....

- Challenge or Lesson Learned:

....

- Plan to Improve Tomorrow:

....

Weekly Reflection

At the end of each week, use this section to track accomplishments and areas needing improvement.

Week #: ....

Weekly Goal Progress:

- Did I accomplish my weekly goal? (Yes/No) ....

- If yes, what contributed to my success? ....

- If no, what held me back? ....

Wins & Milestones:

1. ....

2. ....

3. ....

Challenges Faced:

....

....

Adjustments for Next Week:

....

....

Faith & Focus Check-In:

- Key scripture that sustained me:

....

....

- How did this week bring me closer to fulfilling my vision?

....

....

IMAGINATIVE
(Poiema)

Objective: Unlocking the power of imagination to tap into divine creativity and bring visionary ideas to life.

Key Scripture: Ephesians 2:10

Greek/Hebrew Insight:
Poiema (Greek for "workmanship" or "creation")

Understanding the Power of Imagination

Imagination is a vital component of the prophetic and entrepreneurial process. It allows us to see beyond the physical and enter into the realm of possibility, where God's creativity can flow. Just as God created the heavens and the earth through His words, we are called to imagine and create in partnership with Him.

Unlocking Divine Creativity

Every believer has access to God's creativity, and imagination is the key to unlocking it. God's workmanship (poiema) in us means we are His creative masterpiece, designed to reflect His nature in all we do. This module will explore how to tap into the depths of God's creativity to imagine new possibilities for your life and business.

Shaping Your Vision Through Imagination

Before anything becomes reality, it first exists in the mind. The ability to imagine new opportunities, solutions, and paths is a prophetic gift. By yielding to God's Spirit, you can expand your imagination beyond human limitations, allowing you to envision and bring to life innovative streams of income, new ministries, and fresh business ideas.

Imagination as a Tool for Income Streams

Many entrepreneurs struggle to develop multiple streams of income because they are limited by what they can physically see. This module will help you understand how to use your imagination to see potential opportunities that others might overlook. God's creativity knows no bounds, and neither should your imagination when it comes to creating wealth through biblical principles.

Scenario: The Power of Imagination in Business Innovation

Meet Jessica, an entrepreneur who started Elite Occasions, an event planning business, about five years ago. At first, everything was going well. She was planning weddings, corporate events, private parties—you name it. Clients loved the unique, personal touch she brought to each event, and word of mouth quickly spread.

But after a while, Jessica noticed something troubling: her business had hit a plateau. Revenue wasn't growing like it used to, and competitors were beginning to offer similar services. She started to feel like she was just keeping up, rather than standing out. And as a result, her excitement for the business began to fade.

One day, while reflecting on her situation, it hit her—she wasn't allowing herself to imagine new possibilities for her business. She had fallen into the day-to-day operations and lost sight of the creativity that had made Elite Occasions successful in the first place.

Jessica realized she needed to recapture that imaginative spark. If she wanted to take her business to the next level, she couldn't just stick to what had worked in the past. She had to think bigger, more creatively, and outside the box.

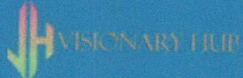

New Ideas Take Shape:

Jessica sat down with a notebook and let her mind run wild. She began to ask herself questions like, "What other services could I offer that would add value to my clients?" and "How can I diversify my income streams without stepping too far away from what I love?"

Soon, she came up with three exciting new ideas:

 Online Event Planning Courses – Teaching others the ropes of the event planning business through an online platform.

 **DIY Party Kits Subscription Box** – A curated box filled with decorations, themes, and guides that people could use to host their own parties at home.

 Corporate Consulting – Offering specialized consulting services to companies looking to create memorable corporate events and internal celebrations.

Mapping Out the Vision

With her new ideas on the table, Jessica didn't waste time. She created a simple vision map that outlined the steps she needed to take for each concept. For the online courses, she researched platforms like Udemy and Teachable. For the subscription box, she began exploring product sourcing and packaging. And for the corporate consulting, she identified a few local companies she could approach for potential partnerships.

It was as if a weight had been lifted. Jessica felt a renewed sense of purpose, and her imagination was driving her toward growth again. She could see how expanding her business in these ways would create multiple streams of income, all while staying true to her passion for events.

Where It Led

Fast forward a year, and Jessica's hard work paid off. She successfully launched her first online course, which became a hit with aspiring event planners. The DIY Party Kits took off too, becoming a favorite for people who wanted to host creative parties at home. The corporate consulting?That opened doors to a whole new network of clients and partnerships. By allowing her imagination to reframe her business, Jessica not only increased her income but also reignited her passion for what she does. She's now positioned as an innovative leader in her industry, all because she dared to dream bigger.

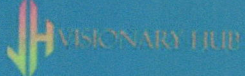

Imaginative (Poiema)

Activity

Creative Idea Generation Exercise:

Take a moment to brainstorm freely and ask yourself: What untapped ideas are lying dormant within me? Write down 2-3 potential new business ventures or income streams that reflect your skills, passions, and market demands. Use this exercise to think beyond your current offerings and explore fresh, creative ideas.

....

....

....

....

....

....

Vision Mapping:

Now that you've generated new ideas, create a vision map that outlines how you can bring these ideas to life. What specific actions will you need to take to transform your imaginative concepts into a functioning business or project? This mapping exercise helps you develop a step-by-step plan to bring your ideas into reality, turning imagination into execution.

....

....

....

....

....

....

Framework 2: IMAGINATIVE

Scripture

"Now unto him that is able to do exceeding abundantly above all that we ask or think, according to the power that worketh in us."
— Ephesians 3:20 (KJV)

What It Means

Imagination propels you to dream beyond your limits. Trust God's power to exceed what you can ask or think.

Reflection Prompt

• What bold dream or idea have you been hesitant to pursue?

....
....
....
....
....

• How can you take one step toward it this week?

....
....
....
....
....

Action Plan for This Week

1. Write down your biggest, most daring idea.
2. Pray for wisdom and insight to act on it.
3. Identify one tangible step to bring that idea closer to reality.

Part 2: Develop Your Strategic Plan (Weeks 2-4)

Objective: Break your vision into actionable steps.

Step 1: Set SMART Goals

For each month:

- **Specific:** What will you accomplish?

- **Measurable:** How will you track progress?

- **Achievable:** Is this realistic in 90 days?

- **Relevant:** Does it align with your overall vision?

- **Time-Bound:** Set clear deadlines.

> **Example:**
> - **Month 1 Goal:** *"Build and launch a marketing funnel for my new product."*
> - **Month 2 Goal:** *"Close $30,000 in sales through targeted campaigns."*
> - **Month 3 Goal:** *"Refine and scale the funnel to reach $50,000."*

Step 2: Weekly Milestones

Break each monthly goal into weekly actions. Use this structure:

- What do I need to accomplish this week?

- Who or what resources can help me?

- What potential challenges might arise?

Daily Planner Template

DATE: /   /

05:00

06:00

07:00

08:00

09:00

10:00

11:00

12:00

13:00

14:00

15:00

16:00

17:00

18:00

19:00

20:00

21:00

22:00

23:00

Top 3 Priorities for the Day

1. ....
2. ....
3. ....

Morning Routine (Set the Tone)

- Scripture/Affirmation of the Day:

- Gratitude List (3 Things):
  1. ....
  2. ....
  3. ....

- Vision Statement: Write down your overarching 90-day vision in one sentence.

....
....
....
....
....

Evening Reflection (Close the Day)

- Biggest Win Today:

....

- Challenge or Lesson Learned:

....

- Plan to Improve Tomorrow:

....

Weekly Reflection

At the end of each week, use this section to track accomplishments and areas needing improvement.

Week #: ....

Weekly Goal Progress:

- Did I accomplish my weekly goal? (Yes/No) ....
- If yes, what contributed to my success? ....
- If no, what held me back? ....

Wins & Milestones:

1. ....
2. ....
3. ....

Challenges Faced:

....

....

Adjustments for Next Week:

....

....

Faith & Focus Check-In:

- Key scripture that sustained me:

....

....

- How did this week bring me closer to fulfilling my vision?

....

....

STRATEGY ORIENTED
(Tachbulah)

Objective: To equip entrepreneurs and corporate leaders with the skills to implement strategic approaches for sustainable growth and financial expansion.

Key Scripture: Proverbs 21:5 – "The plans of the diligent lead to profit as surely as haste leads to poverty."

Greek/Hebrew Insight:
Tachbulah (Hebrew for "strategy" or "guidance") signifies the importance of calculated planning and wisdom in decision-making processes.

The Importance of Strategic Planning

In the world of entrepreneurship and corporate leadership, strategic planning is essential. It allows organizations to set clear goals, allocate resources effectively, and adapt to changing market conditions. Companies that engage in thorough strategic planning are more likely to outperform their competitors.

Example

Every believer has access to God's creativity, and imagination is the key to unlocking it. God's workmanship (poiema) in us means we are His creative masterpiece, designed to reflect His nature in all we do. This module will explore how to tap into the depths of God's creativity to imagine new possibilities for your life and business.

Why Strategic Planning is Crucial

- **Clarity of Purpose:** It helps entrepreneurs clarify their business goals, making it easier to align daily activities with long-term objectives.
- **Risk Mitigation:** A well-thought-out strategy enables leaders to foresee challenges and plan accordingly, minimizing potential risks.
- **Resource Optimization:** Strategic planning ensures that time, talent, and finances are allocated efficiently to maximize output.
- **Adaptability:** A solid strategy allows for flexibility when external factors—like market changes or economic shifts—require quick pivots.

Time Management in Entrepreneurship

Time management is a cornerstone of entrepreneurial success. Entrepreneurs often wear multiple hats and juggle diverse responsibilities such as managing finances, operations, marketing, and growth. Without effective time management, it becomes easy to lose track of critical tasks, leading to missed opportunities and inefficiencies.

Key Strategies for Managing Time:

- **Task Prioritization:** Begin each day by identifying high-priority tasks. These are the actions that directly contribute to revenue generation or business growth. Lower-priority tasks can be delegated or scheduled for later.

- **Calendar Blocking:** Use your calendar to block out dedicated time slots for specific tasks. This prevents interruptions and helps you maintain focus.

- **The 80/20 Rule (Pareto Principle):** Recognize that 80% of your results come from 20% of your efforts. Focus on the activities that drive the most value.

- **Delegation:** Delegate non-essential tasks to team members, freeing up your time to focus on strategy and leadership.

- **Eliminate Time Wasters:** Avoid distractions like excessive meetings, non-essential emails, or social media use during work hours.

Task Prioritization and Scheduling

Managing your schedule efficiently is about more than just time—it's about knowing what to do with that time. As a leader, your role isn't to do everything but to do the most impactful things that drive your vision forward.

Practical Tips for Scheduling and Task Prioritization:

- **Use the Eisenhower Matrix:** Classify tasks into four quadrants: urgent and important, important but not urgent, urgent but not important, and neither urgent nor important. Prioritize tasks accordingly.

- **Batch Similar Tasks:** Group similar activities (e.g., responding to emails, making calls) together to maximize efficiency.

- **Morning vs. Afternoon Workloads:** Schedule the most demanding tasks for times when your energy is highest, often in the morning. Leave less-intensive work for the afternoon.

- **Weekly Reviews:** Set aside time at the end of each week to review your progress and adjust the upcoming week's plan as needed.

- **Scheduling Breaks:** Schedule short breaks to rest and reset. This avoids burnout and improves focus when working on high-level tasks.

Developing a Strategic Action Plan

Successful entrepreneurs don't just dream big—they back their vision with well-executed plans. An action plan bridges the gap between your vision and reality. It provides the steps needed to achieve your goals, enabling you to monitor progress and make adjustments as necessary.

Steps to Creating a Strategic Action Plan

1 **Define Your Vision:** Begin by clearly defining your business's long-term goals. What does success look like? Where do you want your business to be in five years?

....

....

....

....

2 **Conduct a SWOT Analysis:** Evaluate your business's strengths, weaknesses, opportunities, and threats to get a clear understanding of your current position.

3 **Set SMART Goals:** Ensure your objectives are Specific, Measurable, Achievable, Relevant, and Time-bound.

4 **Break Goals into Actionable Steps:** Break down each goal into smaller, actionable tasks. Assign timelines, resources, and personnel to each task. Assign Accountability: If working with a team, delegate responsibilities and establish accountability measures to ensure tasks are completed.

5 **Monitor Progress:** Use KPIs (Key Performance Indicators) to track progress and evaluate success. Be ready to adjust the plan as necessary based on results or changing circumstances.

....

....

....

....

....

....

....

- **Scenario:** John is the CEO of a startup tech company. As his business grows, he finds himself overwhelmed by the sheer number of tasks vying for his attention. Product development, client meetings, marketing strategy, and financial oversight all require his time, but his efforts feel scattered.

- **Solution:** John implements time management strategies. He uses calendar blocking to reserve time each morning for product development (his top priority). He assigns afternoons for meetings and administrative tasks. John also begins delegating client inquiries to his team, allowing him to focus more on strategy.

  As a result, John finds he's more productive, his business runs smoother, and he's able to focus on the bigger picture without getting bogged down by day-to-day tasks.

- **Exercise:** Create Your Strategic Time Management Plan
  Identify Top Priorities: List your top three business priorities for the next quarter. These should directly align with your long-term goals.

  ....
  ....
  ....
  ....

- **Calendar Blocking:** Using your calendar, schedule dedicated time for these priorities. Ensure you block time for strategic thinking and problem-solving as well.

- **Task Delegation:** Identify tasks that can be delegated to team members. Develop a plan to shift those responsibilities.

- **Weekly Check-Ins:** Set up weekly check-ins with yourself or your team to review progress and make necessary adjustments.

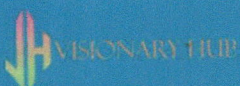

Apple Inc.

Known for its innovative products and disruptive market strategies, Apple is a perfect example of strategic planning in action. Every new product launch is the result of meticulous planning, resource allocation, and precise timing. From the development stage to marketing and distribution, Apple ensures that every step aligns with its larger vision of being a leader in technology.

By focusing on long-term strategy rather than short-term gains, Apple has been able to maintain its competitive edge and continually push the boundaries of innovation.

Conclusion

Successful entrepreneurship and leadership require a well-balanced blend of strategic planning, effective time management, and precise task prioritization. When these elements are in harmony, they provide the necessary structure for sustained growth, profitability, and innovation.

Framework 3: **STRATEGIC MINDSET**

Scripture

"For which of you, intending to build a tower, sitteth not down first, and counteth the cost..." — Luke 14:28 (KJV)

What It Means

Success requires careful planning. Count the cost, organize your resources, and strategize before embarking on any significant endeavor.

Reflection Prompt

- What project are you starting, and have you mapped out the required resources and time?

Action Plan for This Week

1. Break down your goal into clear steps.
2. List the resources needed (time, money, people).
3. Schedule tasks in your Daily Planner.

VISIONARY SMART Goals Chart

Goal	Describe the key outcome you want to achieve.
S (Specific)	Clearly define the goal. Who, what, where, why?
M (Measurable)	Identify specific criteria or metrics to gauge success
A (Achievable)	Ensure the goal is challenging yet attainable with available resources.
R (Relevant)	Confirm the goal aligns with your broader vision or purpose.
T (Time-Bound)	Set a realistic deadline or timeframe for completion

VISIONARY Alignment	
V (Vision-Driven)	In what ways does this goal reflect your long-term vision or calling?
I (Imaginative)	How are you utilizing creativity or fresh ideas to achieve this goal?
S (Strategic Mindset)	Which strategic steps, plans, or frameworks will guide you?
I (Innovative)	Which innovative methods or tools can you implement for a competitive edge?
O (Originator)	How will you differentiate yourself or pioneer a new approach here?
N (Nonconventional)	In what ways can you break the status quo to stand out?
A (Ambitious)	How does this goal push you beyond your comfort zone?
R (Risk-Taker)	What risks must you embrace, and how will you mitigate them?
Y (Yielded to the Process)	How will you remain flexible and adaptable during the journey?

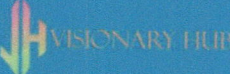

Action Steps

- **Step 1:**

....

- **Step 2:**

....

- **Step 3:**

....

(List out the tasks or milestones necessary to accomplish your goal.)

Resources Needed

Identify any tools, people, or budgets required.

....

....

....

....

Potential Challenges

Note possible roadblocks and outline your plan to address them.

....

....

....

....

Success Indicators

Detail how you'll know you've succeeded. (e.g., numbers, results, feedback)

....

....

....

....

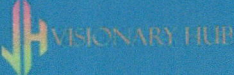

Timeframe

Reiterate your target completion date, plus any milestones.

....

....

....

....

Review & Reflection

Schedule regular check-ins to assess progress, refine action steps, and celebrate milestones.

....

....

....

....

Use this **VISIONARY SMART Goals Chart** as a living document—update it throughout your 90-day journey (or any timeframe). By combining practical goal-setting strategies with a VISIONARY perspective, you'll create goals that are both grounded in detail and fueled by innovation and purpose.

Daily Planner Template

DATE: / /

05:00

06:00

07:00

08:00

09:00

10:00

11:00

12:00

13:00

14:00

15:00

16:00

17:00

18:00

19:00

20:00

21:00

22:00

23:00

Top 3 Priorities for the Day

1. ....
2. ....
3. ....

Morning Routine (Set the Tone)

- Scripture/Affirmation of the Day:
- Gratitude List (3 Things):
  1. ....
  2. ....
  3. ....
- Vision Statement: Write down your overarching 90-day vision in one sentence.

....
....
....
....

Evening Reflection (Close the Day)

- **Biggest Win Today:**

....

- Challenge or Lesson Learned:

....

- Plan to Improve Tomorrow:

....

Weekly Reflection

At the end of each week, use this section to track accomplishments and areas needing improvement.

Week #: ....

Weekly Goal Progress:

- Did I accomplish my weekly goal? (Yes/No) ....
- If yes, what contributed to my success? ....
- If no, what held me back? ....

Wins & Milestones:

1. ....
2. ....
3. ....

Challenges Faced:

....

....

Adjustments for Next Week:

....

....

Faith & Focus Check-In:

- Key scripture that sustained me:

....

....

- How did this week bring me closer to fulfilling my vision?

....

....

INNOVATION
(Chadash)

Introduction:

As a leader or entrepreneur, staying ahead in today's competitive environment requires more than just hard work—it demands innovation. Innovation is about challenging the status quo, finding new ways to solve problems, and consistently delivering value to your customers or clients. This module is designed to help you develop an innovative mindset, guide your strategic planning, and manage your time effectively to bring those new ideas to life.

Understanding Chadash

The Hebrew word Chadash means "new" or "renew," and it's a fitting concept for this module because innovation is all about creating new opportunities. Whether it's developing a fresh product, improving internal processes, or finding a better way to engage customers, innovation means constant renewal and evolution.

In business, Chadash means not settling for what's already working, but continuously seeking ways to improve and adapt. As Steve Jobs once said, "Innovation distinguishes between a leader and a follower." The goal is to be the leader, not the follower.

Innovation in Action

When we think about innovation, companies like Amazon and Tesla come to mind. Their success didn't come from sticking to the status quo—they redefined what's possible in their industries. The same applies to small and growing businesses. Innovation isn't just for tech giants; it's for every entrepreneur who wants to stay competitive, whether you're running a startup, a family business, or scaling a corporate enterprise.

Take the example of Marcus, who owns a small home goods store. He realized that while his products were high-quality, they weren't standing out in a crowded marketplace. Instead of simply trying to out-market his competitors, Marcus decided to innovate by creating an augmented reality (AR) feature on his website. This allowed customers to virtually place products in their homes before purchasing. The result? A surge in sales and customer engagement.

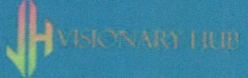

Developing an Innovative Mindset

To foster innovation, you need the right mindset—a blend of curiosity, creativity, and a willingness to embrace failure as part of the process. Here are some key ways to build an innovative mindset:

- **Challenge the Norms:** Don't be afraid to question how things are done. Look for opportunities to break away from traditional approaches.

- **Embrace Risk:** Taking risks is part of the innovation journey. Not every idea will succeed, but each failure provides insight that moves you closer to breakthrough.

- **Stay Curious:** Leaders and entrepreneurs who are constantly learning and exploring new ideas are better equipped to innovate. Stay up-to-date on trends, emerging technologies, and shifts in consumer behavior.

Strategic Innovation Planning

Great ideas are just the beginning. To bring them to life, you need a strategic plan. Successful innovation requires more than creativity—it requires clear goals, timelines, and execution strategies.

- Set Clear Innovation Goals: What specific area do you want to innovate?Is it a new product? A more efficient process? Write down the goal and the problem it solves.

- Develop an Action Plan: Break the innovation process down into manageable steps. What needs to happen first? Who's responsible for each step? How will you measure success?

....

....

....

....

....

....

....

....

....

....

- Prioritize Ideas: Not all innovative ideas should be pursued at once. Use criteria like potential impact, cost, and feasibility to prioritize the ones that will make the most difference.

- Time Management: Block out time in your calendar for innovation. This might mean dedicating time each week to brainstorming or testing new ideas, without getting sidetracked by day-to-day operations.

Time and Task Management for Innovation

Time is a precious resource for every entrepreneur, and managing it effectively is critical for fostering innovation. Here are some strategies to help you focus:

- **Calendar Blocking:** Set aside specific time blocks in your calendar for creative thinking, problem-solving, and developing new ideas. This ensures innovation remains a priority.

- **Task Prioritization:** Use tools like the Eisenhower Matrix to separate urgent tasks from important ones. This helps you focus on long-term innovation rather than getting stuck in the daily grind.

- **Project Management Tools:** Leverage tools like Trello, Asana, or Monday.com to track your innovation projects and ensure you're hitting your milestones.

- **Time Audits:** Review how you're spending your time every week. Are you investing enough in future-focused innovation, or are you constantly in reactive mode?

Exercise: Innovating in Your Business

Here's a simple exercise to jumpstart innovation in your business:

- **Step 1:** Identify a problem in your business or industry. For example, "Our customer onboarding process takes too long and leads to frustration."

- **Step 2:** Brainstorm three innovative ways to solve this problem. Maybe you could automate part of the process, create a self-service platform, or personalize onboarding through AI-driven solutions.

- **Step 3:** Select the most viable option and outline a 3-step action plan for implementing it.

Scenario: Strategic Innovation in Action

- **Scenario:** Emily, the CEO of a mid-sized retail company, realizes that her competitors are beginning to offer similar products at lower prices. Instead of entering a price war, Emily decides to innovate by focusing on enhancing customer experience. She leads her team in developing a loyalty program driven by data analytics, offering personalized rewards based on customer shopping habits.

- **Result:** The new loyalty program increases repeat purchases and customer retention, helping Emily's company stand out in a crowded market. Through innovation, Emily retains her competitive edge without sacrificing profit margins.

Innovation is Creating Something from Nothing

Innovation goes beyond just improving what's already there—it's about bringing entirely new ideas to life, often starting from what feels like nothing. As entrepreneurs and leaders, we're frequently tasked with turning abstract concepts into real-world outcomes, even when the resources are limited, or the road ahead is unclear.

Think about some of the most groundbreaking innovations. The smartphone wasn't just a better phone—it was an entirely new way of integrating technology, communication, and lifestyle. Companies like Airbnb didn't just tweak the hotel industry; they completely reinvented how we think about travel and accommodation, turning spare rooms into valuable assets.

In entrepreneurship, this principle is key. You might face hurdles like tight budgets, saturated markets, or operational roadblocks. But innovation allows you to see opportunities where others might only see obstacles. It's about finding creative ways to reach untapped markets, repurpose resources, or develop new business models that change the game. Creating something from nothing requires vision, creativity, and relentless effort. It's about believing that you can bring value into the world—even if the roadmap doesn't yet exist. Real innovation allows leaders to break new ground and shape industries in ways no one saw coming.

Wrap-up

Innovation is a journey, not a destination. As you lead your organization, commit to continuously pushing the boundaries, finding new ways to deliver value, and disrupting the norm. By fostering an innovative mindset and strategically planning your efforts, you'll ensure long-term success and growth for your business.

Framework 4: **INNOVATIVE**

Scripture

"Cast thy bread upon the waters: for thou shalt find it after many days... Give a portion to seven, and also to eight."
— Ecclesiastes 11:1-2 (KJV)

What It Means

Innovation involves taking calculated risks and diversifying your efforts. Stay adaptable and trust that the return on these risks will come in time.

Reflection Prompt

- Where could you apply a fresh or creative approach?

....

....

....

....

....

- Which new strategy can you try this week?

....

....

....

....

....

Action Plan for This Week

1. Identify one new idea or method to diversify.
2. Commit to experimenting with it.
3. Evaluate the outcome and refine as needed.

Part 3: Innovation and Nonconventional Thinking (Weeks 5-6)

Objective: Challenge yourself to think outside the box and embrace innovative strategies.

Step 1: Identify Opportunities for Innovation

Write down three ways you can do things differently to achieve better results.

- Example: *"Automate my email marketing to save time and increase conversions."*

....

....

....

Step 2: Take a Risk

What bold step can you take that aligns with your vision but challenges your comfort zone?

- Example: *"Pitch my product to five high-profile influencers in my niche."*

....

....

....

Step 3: Mid-Point Reflection

Evaluate progress so far.

- What's working?

....

- What's not working?

....

- What adjustments will you make?

....

Daily Planner Template

Use this page every day for structure and focus.

DATE: /   /

05:00
06:00
07:00
08:00
09:00
10:00
11:00
12:00
13:00
14:00
15:00
16:00
17:00
18:00
19:00
20:00
21:00
22:00
23:00

Top 3 Priorities for the Day

1. ....
2. ....
3. ....

Morning Routine (Set the Tone)

- Scripture/Affirmation of the Day:

- Gratitude List (3 Things):
  1. ....
  2. ....
  3. ....

- Vision Statement: Write down your overarching 90-day vision in one sentence.

....
....
....
....
....

Evening Reflection (Close the Day)

- Biggest Win Today:

....

- Challenge or Lesson Learned:

....

- Plan to Improve Tomorrow:

....

Weekly Reflection

At the end of each week, use this section to track accomplishments and areas needing improvement.

Week #: ....

Weekly Goal Progress:

- Did I accomplish my weekly goal? (Yes/No) ....
- If yes, what contributed to my success? ....
- If no, what held me back? ....

Wins & Milestones:

1. ....
2. ....
3. ....

Challenges Faced:

....

....

Adjustments for Next Week:

....

....

Faith & Focus Check-In:

- Key scripture that sustained me:

....

....

- How did this week bring me closer to fulfilling my vision?

....

....

ORIGINATOR
(Prototokos)

Objective: UTo embrace the role of an originator and initiate new ideas, businesses, and movements, understanding how to lead as a pioneer in both business and thought leadership.

Key Scripture: Colossians 1:15

Prototokos (Greek for "firstborn" or "originator").
The term "Prototokos" embodies the essence of being the first in line, a pioneer. In leadership and entrepreneurship, it emphasizes the importance of creating unique value propositions, thinking outside the box, and taking calculated risks that others may avoid.

The Call to Be an Originator

Every entrepreneur has the potential to pioneer new paths in their industry. Understanding the importance of this role can position you as a market leader rather than a follower.

Biblical and Modern Examples of Originators

Biblical Example:
Joseph in Egypt: By interpreting Pharaoh's dream, Joseph proposed a unique agricultural strategy that prepared Egypt for seven years of famine. His foresight and innovative planning saved countless lives.

Modern Example:
Steve Jobs: His role in creating the iPhone disrupted multiple industries, emphasizing design and user experience, showcasing how innovative thinking can revolutionize markets.

Leadership as an Originator

Successful leaders must be willing to take the initiative in creating new concepts and systems. This requires not only creativity but also resilience to overcome setbacks and learn from failures.

The Originator Mindset in Entrepreneurship

Originators proactively create opportunities rather than waiting for them to arise. This proactive approach is essential for identifying trends and anticipating market shifts.

Cultivating an Environment of Innovation

Foster a workplace culture that encourages creativity. Establish platforms for team brainstorming, open discussions, and feedback to create a safe space for innovative ideas.

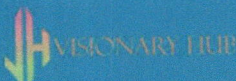

Risk Management and Innovation

Understand that with innovation comes risk. Learn to assess potential risks and develop strategies to mitigate them while pursuing innovative ideas.

Exercises and Prompts:

Exercise 1: Idea Mapping for Innovation

Instructions: List three problems in your industry that remain unsolved. Think critically about issues that frustrate customers or inefficiencies that hinder productivity.

- Problems Proposed Solutions

....

....

....

....

- Brainstorm innovative ideas for each problem:

Problem 1 Solution: ....

Problem 2 Solution: ....

Problem 3 Solution: ....

Exercise 2: Pioneering a New Path

Reflection: Describe a time when you had to act first without a clear roadmap. What challenges did you face, and what did you learn from the experience?

- Experience

....

....

Scenario for Originating New Ideas: Outline how you could originate a new idea or process within your current role or business. Think about how this aligns with your company's mission and vision.

- New Idea/Process: ....

Exercise 3: Market Gap Analysis

Instructions: Identify a gap in the market that isn't currently addressed by competitors. Consider emerging trends, changing consumer preferences, and technological advancements.

- Market Gap: ....

Positioning Yourself: How can you fill that gap? What unique value proposition do you offer?

- Steps to Launch: ....

Exercise 4: Innovation Audit

Instructions: Evaluate your current business or project for its innovative potential. Use the following criteria to assess where improvements can be made. Criteria Current Status Opportunities for Innovation

- Product/Service Quality

....

....

- Customer Experience

....

....

- Operational Efficiency

....

....

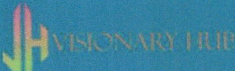

Scenario: Launching a New Product

Imagine you run a small business that sells skincare products. Recently, your customers have been asking for a new all-natural moisturizer, but you're unsure how to develop it.

Prompt: How would you begin the process of creating and launching this new product as an originator?

Action Steps

Market Research: Start by researching what customers are looking for in a natural moisturizer. Are they looking for specific ingredients? What benefits do they expect?

- Customer feedback or trends:

....

Creative Brainstorming: Gather your team (or work solo) to brainstorm ingredients and formulas that would make your product unique. What can set you apart from the competition?

- Unique product ideas:

....

Prototype Development: Create a few sample products based on your research and ideas. Test them with a small group of customers to get feedback.

- Test results and feedback:

....

Marketing Plan: Develop a simple marketing plan to promote the new product. How will you introduce it to your existing customers? What channels will you use to reach new buyers?

- Marketing plan:

....

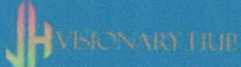

Framework 5: **ORIGINATOR**

Scripture

"In the beginning, God created..."
— Genesis 1:1 (KJV)

What It Means

Being an Originator is about stepping into your role as a creator and leader. You have unique gifts to develop solutions that impact others.

Reflection Prompt

- What is one product or service that only you can bring to life?

....
....
....
....
....

- How does it serve others?

....
....
....
....
....

Action Plan for This Week

1. Outline your unique idea or product.
2. List the first three steps to start creating it.
3. Seek constructive feedback from someone you trust.

Daily Planner Template

DATE: /   /

05:00

06:00

07:00

08:00

09:00

10:00

11:00

12:00

13:00

14:00

15:00

16:00

17:00

18:00

19:00

20:00

21:00

22:00

23:00

Top 3 Priorities for the Day

1. ....
2. ....
3. ....

Morning Routine (Set the Tone)

- Scripture/Affirmation of the Day:

- Gratitude List (3 Things):

  1. ....
  2. ....
  3. ....

- Vision Statement: Write down your overarching 90-day vision in one sentence.

....
....
....
....

Evening Reflection (Close the Day)

- Biggest Win Today:

....

- Challenge or Lesson Learned:

....

- Plan to Improve Tomorrow:

....

Weekly Reflection

Week #: ....

Weekly Goal Progress:

- Did I accomplish my weekly goal? (Yes/No) ....

- If yes, what contributed to my success? ....

- If no, what held me back? ....

Wins & Milestones:

1. ....

2. ....

3. ....

Challenges Faced:

....

....

Adjustments for Next Week:

....

....

Faith & Focus Check-In:

- Key scripture that sustained me:

....

....

- How did this week bring me closer to fulfilling my vision?

....

....

NONCONVENTIONAL
(Paradoxos)

Objective: Embracing nonconventional methods and mindsets for visionary leadership and financial success.

Key Scripture: 1 Corinthians 1:27

Greek/Hebrew Insight:
Paradoxos (Greek for "unexpected" or "unconventional")

Understanding Nonconventional Thinking for Visionaries

Visionaries by nature think differently. They see possibilities where others see limitations, and they're unafraid to disrupt the status quo to achieve a greater goal. Nonconventional thinking is not just an entrepreneurial strategy but a core trait of visionary leadership. Visionaries are often called to step outside the bounds of "normal" to pioneer new paths, whether in business, ministry, or personal development.

As a visionary, your success depends on your ability to create new frameworks, lead in innovative ways, and stay ahead of the curve in your industry or field. Adopting a nonconventional approach allows you to innovate, develop fresh ideas, and provide unique value to those you lead.

Understanding Nonconventional Thinking in Leadership and Entrepreneurship

In the fast-paced world of entrepreneurship, following traditional rules may not always lead to success. Leaders who think nonconventionally break from the pack, choosing creative solutions to seemingly insurmountable challenges. Nonconventional thinkers see opportunities where others see barriers and are willing to take calculated risks that propel them to new levels of achievement.

Think about how many industry disruptors achieved greatness—not by doing what was expected, but by doing what had never been done. If you're too focused on fitting in, your business may plateau or become obsolete in a rapidly changing market.

Look at Uber or Airbnb. Both companies disrupted traditional industries, not by sticking to the old rules, but by adopting fresh approaches. They didn't just compete with taxis or hotels—they created entirely new markets by thinking outside the box.

Now, ask yourself: What could happen if you challenged the norms in your own field? How could you transform your business by exploring an unconventional idea?

Prompt:

Where in your current business or leadership are you sticking to a traditional way of doing things? Write down two areas where you can break away from the usual approach and try something unconventional:

....

....

....

....

Why Being Nonconventional is Essential for Visionary Leaders

Entrepreneurial success is often found in the ability to differentiate yourself. If you follow the crowd, you're just another competitor. But if you innovate and adopt a nonconventional strategy, you can create new markets, generate unique value, and capture the attention of consumers in a saturated marketplace.

Key Consideration: Think about Steve Jobs and Apple. He didn't just design products; he changed how people interact with technology. He took an unconventional approach to everything from marketing to design, which allowed Apple to redefine multiple industries.

Prompt:

Take a moment to consider your industry. Where is there room for disruption? What assumptions could you challenge to open up new opportunities for your business?

....

....

....

....

Scenario: The Startup Challenge

Imagine you run a small tech startup. You've developed a great product, but your customer base isn't growing as fast as you'd hoped. The traditional approach would be to double down on conventional marketing, competing for the same customers as your competitors.

Challenge:

What if, instead, you tried a nonconventional method? Could you target an entirely different demographic, partner with companies in an unexpected way, or use emerging platforms that others are ignoring? What nontraditional approach could you use to reach new customers?How could you redefine your customer experience or value proposition in an innovative way?

....

....

....

....

....

....

- **Analyze Your Current Business:** Identify one area of your business that feels stagnant or too conventional.

....

....

- **Think Creatively:** List three ways you could disrupt the traditional approach in your industry or redefine how your business operates.

....

....

- **Action Plan:** Choose one idea and create a 30-day action plan to test this new, nonconventional strategy.

....

....

Time Management in Nonconventional Strategies

When you embrace nonconventional strategies, managing your time becomes even more important. These new methods often require experimentation, and if you're not disciplined in your scheduling, it's easy to lose focus.

Key Tips:

- **Block Time for Innovation:** Set aside specific hours each week dedicated solely to brainstorming or working on new, nontraditional ideas.

- **Prioritize What Works:** Once you start implementing nonconventional strategies, be ruthless about cutting what doesn't work and doubling down on what does.

- **Track Your Progress:** Use task management tools or a journal to keep track of what's working and what needs adjustment.

Prompt:

Identify three tasks you can delegate or automate to free up more time for developing nonconventional ideas.

....

....

....

....

....

....

....

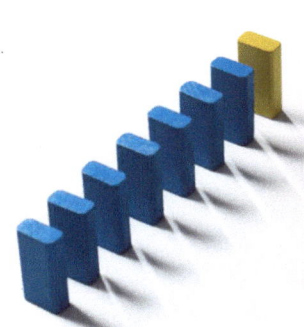

Wrap-up

As a leader or entrepreneur, adopting nonconventional strategies doesn't mean abandoning all the rules—it means being willing to reimagine them. By challenging the norm and seeking innovative solutions, you open the door to new opportunities, stronger market positions, and long-term success.

Daily Planner Template

Use this page every day for structure and focus.

DATE: ___ / ___ / ___

05:00	
06:00	
07:00	
08:00	
09:00	
10:00	
11:00	
12:00	
13:00	
14:00	
15:00	
16:00	
17:00	
18:00	
19:00	
20:00	
21:00	
22:00	
23:00	

Top 3 Priorities for the Day

1. ....
2. ....
3. ....

Morning Routine (Set the Tone)

- Scripture/Affirmation of the Day:

- Gratitude List (3 Things):
  1. ....
  2. ....
  3. ....

- Vision Statement: Write down your overarching 90-day vision in one sentence.

....

....

....

....

Evening Reflection (Close the Day)

- Biggest Win Today:

....

- Challenge or Lesson Learned:

....

- Plan to Improve Tomorrow:

....

Daily Planner Template

DATE: /   /

05:00

06:00

07:00

08:00

09:00

10:00

11:00

12:00

13:00

14:00

15:00

16:00

17:00

18:00

19:00

20:00

21:00

22:00

23:00

Top 3 Priorities for the Day

1. ....
2. ....
3. ....

Morning Routine (Set the Tone)

- Scripture/Affirmation of the Day:

- Gratitude List (3 Things):
  1. ....
  2. ....
  3. ....

- Vision Statement: Write down your overarching 90-day vision in one sentence.

....
....
....
....

Evening Reflection (Close the Day)

- Biggest Win Today:

....

- Challenge or Lesson Learned:

....

- Plan to Improve Tomorrow:

....

Weekly Reflection

At the end of each week, use this section to track accomplishments and areas needing improvement.

Week #: ....

Weekly Goal Progress:

- Did I accomplish my weekly goal? (Yes/No) ....
- If yes, what contributed to my success? ....
- If no, what held me back? ....

Wins & Milestones:

1. ....
2. ....
3. ....

Challenges Faced:

....

....

Adjustments for Next Week:

....

....

Faith & Focus Check-In:

- Key scripture that sustained me:

....

....

- How did this week bring me closer to fulfilling my vision?

....

....

AMBITION
(Philotimia)

Objective: Pursuing excellence and striving for meaningful goals in business, leadership, and life with a mindset of diligence and purpose, aligning ambition with God's will.

Key Scripture: Colossians 3:23 (NIV) – "Whatever you do, work at it with all your heart, as working for the Lord, not for human masters."

Greek/Hebrew Insight:
Philotimia (φιλοτιμία) – A Greek word meaning "love of honor" or "ambition," often used to describe an eager pursuit of noble goals with integrity and dedication.

Ambition in Leadership and Entrepreneurship

In today's fast-changing world of business, having a strong sense of ambition is essential for any leader. As industries evolve, customer preferences shift, and new opportunities emerge, successful leaders are those who remain driven and committed to growth. Without ambition, even the most promising ventures can lose momentum and fall behind.

True ambition isn't about chasing success blindly—it's about pursuing meaningful goals with dedication and integrity, all while staying true to your core values. The Bible reminds us in Colossians 3:23 to put our whole heart into everything we do, working as if for the Lord. Effective leaders keep their eyes on their goals, remain adaptable, and seize opportunities that align with their greater mission.

Scenario

Imagine you're the CEO of a small tech company that specializes in developing mobile apps for retail businesses.** For years, your company has been successful in building custom apps, but you've identified a new opportunity: the rise of no-code platforms that empower businesses to create their own apps with ease. Instead of seeing this trend as a threat, your ambition drives you to seize it as a chance to expand and lead in a rapidly evolving market.

You have two choices: stay within your comfort zone and continue offering custom solutions, or channel your ambition to innovate and dominate this emerging space.

Pursuing ambition in this scenario could mean proactively upskilling your team, investing in R&D to create unique add-ons for no-code platforms, or launching strategic partnerships that position your company as a leader in no-code solutions. Taking bold steps may require calculated risks and stepping into unfamiliar territory, but without ambition, your business could miss out on a transformational growth opportunity.

Prompt:

In your current business or leadership role, where do you see opportunities to pursue greater ambition? What market shifts or emerging trends are signaling that it's time to take bold steps toward growth and innovation?

....

....

....

....

....

....

....

....

....

....

Knowing When to Strive for More

A key trait of anyone looking to grow—whether in business, leadership, or personal life—is recognizing when it's time to push beyond the familiar and embrace new opportunities. Sticking with the same routines or approaches when they no longer bring results can hold back progress. Striving for more doesn't mean losing sight of what matters most—it means refining your approach to unlock new possibilities and tackle fresh challenges.

Signs It Might Be Time to Reach Higher:

- **Shifting Needs and Priorities:** If what once worked no longer brings the same fulfillment or success, it might be time to explore new strategies that better align with your goals.

- **Changing Environment:** Whether in your career, community, or personal life, staying adaptable and open to new ideas can help you remain relevant and impactful.

- **Feeling Stuck:** If progress has slowed, it may be the perfect moment to reassess your direction, set new goals, and take bold steps toward growth.

Recognizing these signs and embracing change with confidence can open the door to new opportunities and long-term success in any area of life..

Example of Ambition in Action:
Netflix began as a DVD rental company, but their ambition to lead in the entertainment industry pushed them to evolve. As streaming technology advanced and customer preferences shifted toward on-demand content, they seized the opportunity to innovate. Instead of remaining in their comfort zone, they embraced change and transformed into one of the world's largest streaming platforms. Their bold decision to pursue greater possibilities propelled them to sustained success and industry leadership.

Exercise:

- List three areas in your life or leadership role where you see opportunities to reach new heights:

....

....

....

....

- What bold actions or new possibilities could you explore to elevate your impact?

....

....

....

....

Pursuing Greater Ambition in Life and Leadership

Ambition isn't just about making significant changes; it's about striving for excellence in all aspects of your life. Ambitious individuals understand that while having a long-term vision is crucial, taking meaningful steps every day toward improvement is what truly drives growth.

In ministry or community leadership, ambition might mean recognizing how the needs of those you serve have evolved. What worked before may no longer serve them the best, and ambitious leadership means seeking innovative solutions to meet those changing needs. In your personal life, this could involve setting new goals, embracing challenges, or refining your habits to maximize personal growth and well-being

Imagine you're someone who thrives in face-to-face interactions, whether in teaching, coaching, or community building. When the pandemic caused restrictions, you had to quickly adapt to virtual meetings. While the change was initially challenging, you discovered that it expanded your reach and allowed you to connect with more people than you could have before. Now, you face a decision: return to in-person interactions, continue focusing on virtual engagements, or blend both in a new way.

An ambitious approach here would involve combining the best of both worlds—continuing to offer in-person connections where they matter most, while embracing the wider opportunities that come with virtual engagement to reach and inspire a broader community.

Exercise:

- Reflect on a recent situation where pursuing a bold new direction was necessary. How did you approach it, and what were the results?
  Identify two areas in your current life or leadership role where a more ambitious approach could drive greater success or growth for your team or operations:

....

....

....

....

....

....

....

....

....

....

Embracing Ambition and Transformation

The Greek word "Philotimia" reflects the concept of ambition—a deep desire to achieve excellence and pursue meaningful success. It embodies the drive to push beyond the ordinary, seek out new opportunities, and make transformative progress in various areas of life. Whether in personal growth, leadership, or community involvement, ambition serves as the force that propels individuals to rise to their potential, no matter the obstacles.

Perspective on Ambition:

Ambition is not just about striving for external success; it's about cultivating a mindset that challenges you to constantly grow, evolve, and make a positive impact in the world around you. This mindset can show up in many areas of our everyday lives: striving to improve in our careers, learning new skills, building stronger relationships, or contributing to our communities.

Ambition leads to a deeper sense of purpose and fulfillment, encouraging you to take bold steps toward your goals—even when faced with challenges. It's about recognizing opportunities for growth and daring to pursue them, whether it's taking on a new project at work, deciding to further your education, or pushing through personal setbacks to achieve a healthier lifestyle.

You run a local clothing boutique that has enjoyed success for several years, but recently, sales have stagnated. After some research, you realize that your customer base has shifted toward online shopping, and there is a growing demand for eco-friendly fashion. Instead of sticking to the old model, you embrace the ambition to innovate and decide to launch an online platform featuring a sustainable clothing line. This new direction opens up fresh possibilities for connecting with a broader audience, ultimately reigniting growth and success for your business.

In our personal lives, ambition could look like setting a fitness goal, starting a side project, or dedicating time to learning something new that excites you. Whether in work, relationships, or self-improvement, ambition is the key to pushing forward and finding fulfillment through continuous growth.

Exercise 1: Identify Areas for Bold Growth

- Identify one area in your life, career, or leadership role where you feel the drive to pursue greater ambition. Write down why you believe this area holds potential for growth.

....

....

....

- What bold steps can you take to pursue this ambition? Break it down into actionable steps:

....

....

....

Exercise 2: Create an Ambition Action Plan

- Reflect on an area where you've been hesitant to push yourself further. Write down what has been holding you back from pursuing greater ambition in this area: Now, create a plan to take bold action toward your goal. Include specific steps, a timeline for achieving them, and identify resources or support that can help propel you forward:

....

....

....

Ambition is the cornerstone of sustainable leadership and personal growth.It's about recognizing the potential for transformation and seeking new opportunities to achieve greatness. Whether you're adapting to changing circumstances, embracing new challenges, or shifting your approach to reach higher goals, ambition is what drives long-term success. The challenge lies not only in identifying those opportunities but in taking decisive steps to pursue them, even when they push you beyond your comfort zone. Ambition fuels growth, empowers you to overcome obstacles, and enables you to lead with vision and purpose.

Framework 7: AMBITIOUS

Scripture

"I press toward the mark for the prize of the high calling…"
— Philippians 3:14 (KJV)

What It Means

Godly ambition drives you to pursue excellence aligned with your calling. Keep pushing forward, trusting that your efforts lead to a greater impact.

Reflection Prompt

• What significant goal are you working toward now?

....
....
....
....
....

• How does it align with your higher calling?

....
....
....
....
....

Action Plan for This Week

1. Write down a major goal that energizes you.
2. Identify obstacles and strategize overcoming them.
3. Take one bold action step this week to move closer to that goal.

Part 4: **Accelerate Ambition and Results (Weeks 7-8)**

Step 1: Amplify What's Working

Focus on the 20% of actions generating 80% of results. Write them down and plan to scale them.

....

....

....

....

Step 2: Remove Barriers

Identify time-wasters or obstacles and create a plan to eliminate them.

- Example: *"Outsource customer support to free up 10 hours per week for sales calls."*

....

....

....

....

Step 3: Build Momentum

Identify one high-impact action to take this week to propel you closer to your 90-day goal.

....

....

....

....

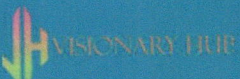

Daily Planner Template

Use this page every day for structure and focus.

DATE: _____ / _____ / _____

05:00	
06:00	
07:00	
08:00	
09:00	
10:00	
11:00	
12:00	
13:00	
14:00	
15:00	
16:00	
17:00	
18:00	
19:00	
20:00	
21:00	
22:00	
23:00	

Top 3 Priorities for the Day

1. ....
2. ....
3. ....

Morning Routine (Set the Tone)

- Scripture/Affirmation of the Day:
- Gratitude List (3 Things):
  1. ....
  2. ....
  3. ....
- Vision Statement: Write down your overarching 90-day vision in one sentence.

....
....
....
....
....

Evening Reflection (Close the Day)

- Biggest Win Today:

....

- Challenge or Lesson Learned:

....

- Plan to Improve Tomorrow:

....

Weekly Reflection

At the end of each week, use this section to track accomplishments and areas needing improvement.

Week #: ....

Weekly Goal Progress:

- Did I accomplish my weekly goal? (Yes/No) ....
- If yes, what contributed to my success? ....
- If no, what held me back? ....

Wins & Milestones:

1. ....
2. ....
3. ....

Challenges Faced:

....

....

Adjustments for Next Week:

....

....

Faith & Focus Check-In:

- Key scripture that sustained me:

....

....

- How did this week bring me closer to fulfilling my vision?

....

....

RISK TAKER
(Safar)

Objective: Develop the courage and discernment to take calculated risks that align with your vision and propel your business or leadership forward.

Key Scripture: 2 Timothy 1:7 (NIV) – "For the Spirit God gave us does not make us timid, but gives us power, love, and self-discipline."

Greek/Hebrew Insight:
Safar (to count, measure, or recount opportunities).

The Necessity of Risk in Leadership and Business

In leadership and entrepreneurship, playing it safe often leads to stagnation. To innovate, grow, and reach new heights, we must be willing to take risks. Whether launching a new product, entering new markets, or scaling up operations, each decision involves uncertainty. However, it's often in those risks that we discover breakthroughs.

The Hebrew word Safar speaks to the idea of assessing or "counting" the cost. Risk-takers aren't careless; they carefully consider opportunities and challenges. In the business world, calculated risks lead to big rewards when done with the right balance of faith, wisdom, and preparation.

Example:
Think of successful entrepreneurs like Elon Musk or Richard Branson, who took risks that led to innovations that revolutionized industries. Their courage to step into uncharted waters paid off in massive ways.

The Power and Reward of Taking Risks

Understanding the Importance of Risk-Taking

Taking risks is a fundamental aspect of growth and progress in leadership and entrepreneurship. When you embrace the unknown, you open yourself up to possibilities that can lead to remarkable achievements and innovations. Here's a closer look at the power of risk-taking and the rewards that come with it.

The Power of Taking Risks

- **Catalyst for Innovation:** Risks are often the precursor to innovation. By stepping outside of your comfort zone, you challenge the status quo and encourage creative thinking. For instance, when Netflix decided to pivot from DVD rentals to streaming services, it took a significant risk that ultimately transformed the entertainment industry.

- **Building Resilience:** Engaging in risk-taking fosters resilience. Each risk, regardless of its outcome, serves as a learning opportunity. The lessons learned from both successes and failures contribute to your growth as a leader and entrepreneur. This resilience prepares you to face future challenges with confidence.

- **Confidence and Leadership Development:** Leaders who take calculated risks tend to inspire those around them. When you make bold decisions, you not only gain respect but also foster a culture of courage and innovation within your team. Your willingness to embrace uncertainty sets a powerful example for others to follow.

- **Uncovering New Opportunities:** Often, significant opportunities lie just beyond the edge of risk. Whether it's entering a new market, launching a groundbreaking product, or changing your business model, taking the leap can lead to unexpected and fruitful outcomes. Being open to risk allows you to discover paths you might not have considered otherwise.

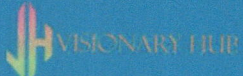

The Rewards of Taking Risks

- **Accelerated Growth:** Companies that embrace risk often experience rapid growth. By venturing into new markets or developing innovative products, they can expand their reach and influence. A prime example is Apple, which consistently took risks with its product lines, resulting in substantial growth and market leadership.

- **Financial Gains:** Taking risks can lead to substantial financial rewards. Successful ventures often result in increased revenue and profitability. For example, when a small business decides to invest in new technology or marketing strategies, the potential for high returns can far outweigh the initial costs.

- **Market Differentiation:** Risk-takers can set themselves apart in competitive markets. By offering unique solutions or services that others shy away from, businesses can carve out a niche and attract loyal customers. This differentiation often translates into a strong brand presence and customer loyalty.

- **Legacy and Influence:** Bold leaders who take risks leave a lasting legacy. Their willingness to innovate and challenge norms not only shapes their organizations but also influences entire industries. These leaders are remembered for their courage and vision, inspiring future generations of entrepreneurs.

In summary, taking risks is not just about the potential for failure; it's about the incredible opportunities for growth and success that come with it. The power of risk-taking lies in its ability to catalyze innovation, build resilience, and unlock new avenues for financial success. As a leader or entrepreneur, embracing risk is essential for achieving your vision and making a meaningful impact in your field.

Framework 8: RISK TAKER

Scripture

"But without faith it is impossible to please him…"
— Hebrews 11:6 (KJV)

What It Means

Being a Risk Taker involves stepping out in faith. God honors diligence and boldness, rewarding those who trust in Him rather than their own comfort zones.

Reflection Prompt

● In what area of your life or business have you been hesitant to take a leap of faith?

....
....
....
....
....

● What will it look like to trust God in this area?

....
....
....
....
....

Action Plan for This Week

1. Identify a specific risk that aligns with your goals and faith.
2. Pray for courage and clarity.
3. Take the first step toward that risk and observe how God meets you there.

Daily Planner Template

DATE: /   /

05:00

06:00

07:00

08:00

09:00

10:00

11:00

12:00

13:00

14:00

15:00

16:00

17:00

18:00

19:00

20:00

21:00

22:00

23:00

Top 3 Priorities for the Day

1. ....

2. ....

3. ....

Morning Routine (Set the Tone)

- Scripture/Affirmation of the Day:

- Gratitude List (3 Things):

    1. ....

    2. ....

    3. ....

- Vision Statement: Write down your overarching 90-day vision in one sentence.

Evening Reflection (Close the Day)

- Biggest Win Today:

- Challenge or Lesson Learned:

- Plan to Improve Tomorrow:

Weekly Reflection

Week #: ....

Weekly Goal Progress:

- Did I accomplish my weekly goal? (Yes/No) ....
- If yes, what contributed to my success? ....
- If no, what held me back? ....

Wins & Milestones:

1. ....
2. ....
3. ....

Challenges Faced:

....

....

Adjustments for Next Week:

....

....

Faith & Focus Check-In:

- Key scripture that sustained me:

....

....

- How did this week bring me closer to fulfilling my vision?

....

....

YIELDING TO THE PROCESS

(Natan)

Objective: To guide you to embrace the process that God has set before you. Each exercise will help you to explore patience, trust, endurance, and faith, ensuring you're equipped for a fulfilling journey that honors God's plan.

Key Scripture: To everything there is a season, A time for every purpose under heaven." - Ecclesiastes 3:1 (NKJV)

Greek/Hebrew Insight:
Natan — to give, to yield. In Hebrew, Natan signifies an intentional act of surrender to a higher purpose. Yielding is a conscious choice to release control and trust God's plan, knowing that He is working every stage for our good and growth.

Example: Imagine an entrepreneur who has poured years of hard work into a business. When an unexpected downturn strikes, they face the choice of either doubling down with control and anxiety or yielding to the process, trusting that this challenge could bring growth in ways they hadn't anticipated. By choosing to natan, or yield, they take a step back, reassess their approach, and seek new solutions. This openness to adapt allows them to innovate, perhaps discovering a new market or refining their product in a way that ultimately makes the business stronger. Yielding doesn't mean giving up; it's an intentional act of trusting the process, remaining flexible, and allowing unforeseen challenges to shape a better path forward.

In every journey of growth and vision, there is a crucial element often overlooked: the necessity to yield. Yielding to the process is about surrendering to God's divine timing, embracing each stage of growth, and learning from every challenge. This is not simply a passive waiting but an active choice to trust, grow, and endure. When we yield, we allow God's wisdom and purpose to shape us beyond what we could achieve on our own. Yielding to the process protects us from what's known as arrested development—a halting of growth due to impatience, fear, or resistance. Rather than stalling or skipping essential steps, yielding teaches us to lean into God's plan, trusting that every season, whether one of joy or challenge, has a purpose. It transforms us, building the strength and wisdom needed to fulfill our vision.

In this section, we will explore how to yield with intention, embracing growth in stages, trusting God's timing, and finding value in every challenge. Each principle within the V.I.S.I.O.N.A.R.Y. framework equips you to live out your purpose with resilience, peace, and a commitment to God's timing. By yielding, you open yourself to the fullness of God's guidance, setting a foundation for lasting transformation and a legacy of faith.

Let this journey of yielding be one of intentional surrender and strength, where each step brings you closer to the person and purpose God has called you to become.

Embracing Yielding as a Strategic Choice

Yielding to the process is a proactive decision to let go of rigid control and allow experiences, challenges, and time to shape your growth and effectiveness as a leader. Yielding isn't about passivity; it's an active choice to be open, adaptable, and purpose-driven, knowing that true progress often requires patience and flexibility. Leaders who yield understand that every stage has lessons, and they remain open to shifts in direction. Yielding to the process also builds emotional intelligence and keeps leaders from burnout, fostering a healthier, more sustainable leadership journey.

Exercise: Reframing Yielding

- Reflect on your own perception of yielding. Do you see it as a loss of control, or can it become a strength in your leadership style? Write a paragraph on how yielding might actually enhance your effectiveness and help your team thrive.

....
....
....
....

Action Plan:

- List three areas in your life where yielding (or practicing flexibility) could benefit you. For each, write what releasing control might look like and any positive outcomes you expect to see, such as reduced stress, increased creativity, or enhanced problem-solving.

....
....
....

Recognizing the Value of Every Stage of Life

Each phase of life, whether it's a season of joy, waiting, or struggle, is a critical part of our journey, custom-designed to stretch us, teach us, and ultimately shape us. When we recognize that every experience has its own timing and purpose, we begin to see each phase as a building block for resilience and wisdom. By embracing each moment, rather than rushing to the next chapter, we allow ourselves the chance to grow in ways that only this season can offer.

Yielding to the present moment doesn't mean giving up control, but rather actively trusting that there's a reason behind every phase. This mindset shift transforms each experience, even the difficult ones, into opportunities for growth, empathy, and deeper self-awareness. When we rush past these moments, we miss out on crucial insights—pieces of wisdom that can only be gained by immersing ourselves fully in the process.

Learning to yield allows us to absorb life's lessons deeply. It's through this yielding that we gain insight and perspective, connecting the dots between where we've been and where we're going. Every phase, when lived fully, builds a foundation that strengthens us, positioning us for the next stage with greater clarity and preparedness. In this way, each chapter becomes more than an isolated experience; it becomes part of a cohesive story that prepares us for our future, equipping us with the strength, patience, and wisdom we'll need for what lies ahead.

Exercise: Stage Reflection

- Think about a recent phase in your life. Was it a time of happiness, growth, waiting, or challenge? Write down the lessons you learned and how this stage helped you grow.

....

....

....

....

....

Avoiding the Trap of Short-Term Thinking

Short-term thinking can result in arrested development, where personal growth is halted due to impatience or fear. Yielding to the process helps you resist the urge for instant gratification, allowing for lasting, meaningful progress. When you focus on growth over immediate results, you become more adaptable and better prepared for the future.

Patience prevents us from stalling our own development. When we yield to long-term growth, we develop greater resilience and mental flexibility, avoiding burnout and achieving more meaningful success.

Embracing Challenges as Growth Opportunities

Challenges often arrive uninvited, yet they are some of the most profound and enduring teachers we encounter. Yielding to challenges doesn't imply surrender; rather, it's a shift in perspective—a willingness to see them as opportunities to stretch ourselves beyond what we thought possible. When we choose to embrace these difficult moments, we build inner strength, adaptability, and resourcefulness. We learn to think creatively, find new solutions, and navigate setbacks with a sense of purpose, equipping us with the tools we need not just to survive, but to thrive in the face of future obstacles.

When we approach challenges with a growth mindset, we give ourselves permission to see failure not as a dead end, but as a stepping stone on the path to wisdom and resilience. Each challenge teaches us invaluable lessons about ourselves and our capacities, reinforcing our confidence. With every hurdle we overcome, we add to a growing foundation of resilience and self-belief that prepares us for greater and more complex trials ahead.

By yielding to challenges in this way, we nurture an attitude of openness, seeing obstacles not as roadblocks but as essential parts of our journey toward personal growth. This outlook grounds us in the present and helps us remain optimistic, even when the road is difficult. It reminds us that challenges don't define our limitations; they reveal our hidden strengths, drawing out our potential and deepening our wisdom. When we yield to challenges, we allow them to mold us into more resilient, confident, and grounded individuals, ready to face whatever comes next with grace and strength.

Cultivating Patience and Trust in Timing

Cultivating patience and trusting in the timing of your journey requires a shift in perspective—from wanting immediate results to appreciating the gradual unfolding of life. Living with patience is an acknowledgment that true growth, whether in personal development, relationships, or career aspirations, is a journey rather than a sprint. Each step is an opportunity to learn, evolve, and refine our goals and desires, and by allowing these to mature naturally, we establish a steady, enduring foundation.

Trusting in life's timing means recognizing that things will manifest at the right moment and that each delay or redirection has its purpose. Often, this is where ideas strengthen, relationships deepen, and goals become clearer and more aligned with who we truly are.

Yielding to timing is an act of faith in the process, a belief that everything has its season and that rushing only undermines the quality of what's yet to come. It provides a sense of stability, allowing us to move forward with intention rather than impulse.

Patience also cultivates resilience. By embracing each stage of our journey, even the waiting periods, we become more adaptable and open to life's ebbs and flows. This resilience fosters a sense of balance, where we can find contentment in meaningful progress rather than being driven solely by the desire for immediate results. As we practice yielding to timing, we become more mindful, present, and engaged in our experiences, trusting that each moment is contributing to our well-being and future success.

In a world that often prioritizes speed and instant gratification, choosing patience is a form of self-care. It allows us to slow down, focus on what truly matters, and nurture a sense of inner peace. This habit of trust helps us approach life with calmness and confidence, knowing that every phase has its role in preparing us for what lies ahead. With patience, we're better able to celebrate small victories, appreciate each lesson, and find fulfillment in the journey itself, making us ready for the bigger picture when it arrives.

Celebrating Small Wins to Build Momentum

Celebrating small wins is a powerful tool for sustaining motivation and building momentum in personal growth. These small victories, however minor they may seem, are stepping stones that create a sense of accomplishment, reinforcing the progress you're making along the way. When we take the time to acknowledge these moments, we not only boost our morale but also gain a clearer perspective on the cumulative effect of our efforts. Each win, however small, becomes a reminder of our growth and resilience, providing fuel to keep us moving forward with a positive mindset.

Yielding to the process by appreciating every incremental step helps us stay present and mindful of the journey itself. It's easy to get fixated on long-term goals and overlook the day-to-day progress that leads to those big achievements. But by valuing each small victory, we remain grounded and connected to the process, which can deepen our sense of purpose and satisfaction. Each step forward, however small, builds our belief in our abilities, showing us that we are indeed capable of growth and success.

Recognizing small wins also helps prevent burnout. When we allow ourselves to pause and celebrate our efforts, we create space to recharge and maintain enthusiasm for what's next. Small wins act as checkpoints along the journey, where we can reflect on the challenges we've overcome and the new skills we've acquired. This acknowledgment of progress acts as a mental reset, keeping us resilient, motivated, and ready for the next phase with renewed energy.

Moreover, celebrating small wins builds a habit of positivity. As we accumulate these moments of success, we cultivate a mindset that is attuned to noticing growth rather than focusing solely on gaps or shortcomings. This positive momentum not only helps us move forward with confidence but also reinforces a cycle of continual achievement. Each small victory becomes a building block, empowering us to reach higher, push further, and embrace the journey with an open heart, knowing that every step we take, however modest, is bringing us closer to our larger goals.

Yielding to the process is a journey of patience, growth, and self-discovery. It requires adaptability, resilience, and a commitment to learning from each step along the way. This approach allows you to live with greater intention, embrace change, and create a more fulfilling life.

Reflection Questions

- How has this approach to yielding changed your perspective on personal growth?

....

....

....

- Are there specific areas where you find yielding challenging? What steps can you take to overcome these challenges?

....

....

....

- What new goals will you set to practice patience, adaptability, and resilience in your personal journey?

....

....

....

Commitment Statement:

- Write a personal commitment statement summarizing your desire to yield to the process. Include a key insight, affirmation, or intention that resonates with you as you continue this journey of growth and self-discovery.

....

....

....

....

....

....

....

Framework 9: **YIELDED**

Scripture

"Trust in the Lord with all thine heart; and lean not unto thine own understanding..." — Proverbs 3:5-6 (KJV)

What It Means

Yielding to God means releasing control and trusting His greater plan. When you acknowledge God's sovereignty in all your ways, He directs your path to true success.

Reflection Prompt

- Which situation are you still trying to control?

....

....

....

....

....

- How can you surrender and acknowledge God more fully?

....

....

....

....

Action Plan for This Week

1. Pick one area where you need to yield control.
2. Spend intentional time in prayer or meditation, inviting God to direct you.
3. Follow the guidance or confirmation you receive, trusting His timing and plan.

Part 5: Yield to the Process (Weeks 9-10)

Objective: Trust God's timing and embrace perseverance.

Step 1: Prayer and Reflection

Spend time in prayer, asking for wisdom and clarity. Write down insights or directions you feel led to take.

Step 2: Embrace Challenges

List the biggest challenges you've faced and how they've helped you grow.

Step 3: Refocus on Faith

Write a declaration of faith:

- Example: *"I trust God to guide me and bless my efforts. I am walking in purpose and fulfilling my calling."*

Daily Planner Template

DATE: /   /

05:00

06:00

07:00

08:00

09:00

10:00

11:00

12:00

13:00

14:00

15:00

16:00

17:00

18:00

19:00

20:00

21:00

22:00

23:00

Top 3 Priorities for the Day

1. ....

2. ....

3. ....

Morning Routine (Set the Tone)

- Scripture/Affirmation of the Day:

- Gratitude List (3 Things):

    1. ....

    2. ....

    3. ....

- Vision Statement: Write down your overarching 90-day vision in one sentence.

....

....

....

....

....

Evening Reflection (Close the Day)

- Biggest Win Today:

....

- Challenge or Lesson Learned:

....

- Plan to Improve Tomorrow:

....

Weekly Reflection

At the end of each week, use this section to track accomplishments and areas needing improvement.

Week #: ....

Weekly Goal Progress:

- Did I accomplish my weekly goal? (Yes/No) ....
- If yes, what contributed to my success? ....
- If no, what held me back? ....

Wins & Milestones:

1. ....
2. ....
3. ....

Challenges Faced:

....

....

Adjustments for Next Week:

....

....

Faith & Focus Check-In:

- Key scripture that sustained me:

....

....

- How did this week bring me closer to fulfilling my vision?

....

....

Conclusion and Next Steps

Your 90-Day Journey

Congratulations on completing this 90-Day V.I.S.I.O.N.A.R.Y Workbook! You have taken significant steps to clarify your vision, align your daily actions with Kingdom principles, and establish a foundation for lasting success.

Key Reminders

1. Continue using the **Daily Planner** to maintain discipline and direction.
2. Reflect weekly, celebrating wins and adjusting where needed.
3. Embrace each of the **9 Frameworks** as a lifelong practice, not just a 90-day sprint.

Consider Ongoing Support

- **One-on-One Coaching:** For deeper, personalized guidance.
- **Group Mastermind:** Join a community of like-minded entrepreneurs.
- **Online Courses & Resources:** Explore expanded trainings that further develop your Kingdom entrepreneurship skills.

Final Word

As you move forward, remember that success is not solely about profits—it's about living out your God-given purpose, serving others, and leaving a legacy that honors Him. Stay committed, stay faithful, and stay expectant of what God will do in and through your life.

"Now unto him that is able to do exceeding abundantly above all that we ask or think..." — Ephesians 3:20

Part 6: **Celebrate and Scale (Weeks 11-12)**

Objective: Achieve your 90-day goal and plan for continued success.

Step 1: Measure Success

Did you achieve your goal? If yes, celebrate! If not, identify areas for growth and improvement.

....

....

....

....

....

Step 2: Plan for the Next 90 Days

What's your next big goal? How will you build on your success?

....

....

....

....

....

Step 3: Gratitude and Legacy

Write down three things you're grateful for and how this experience has impacted your legacy.

....

....

....

....

....

Daily Planner Template

DATE: / /

05:00

06:00

07:00

08:00

09:00

10:00

11:00

12:00

13:00

14:00

15:00

16:00

17:00

18:00

19:00

20:00

21:00

22:00

23:00

Top 3 Priorities for the Day

1. ....
2. ....
3. ....

Morning Routine (Set the Tone)

- Scripture/Affirmation of the Day:
- Gratitude List (3 Things):
  1. ....
  2. ....
  3. ....
- Vision Statement: Write down your overarching 90-day vision in one sentence.

....
....
....
....
....

Evening Reflection (Close the Day)

- Biggest Win Today:

....

- Challenge or Lesson Learned:

....

- Plan to Improve Tomorrow:

....

Weekly Reflection

At the end of each week, use this section to track accomplishments and areas needing improvement.

Week #: ....

Weekly Goal Progress:

- Did I accomplish my weekly goal? (Yes/No) ....
- If yes, what contributed to my success? ....
- If no, what held me back? ....

Wins & Milestones:

1. ....
2. ....
3. ....

Challenges Faced:

....

....

Adjustments for Next Week:

....

....

Faith & Focus Check-In:

- Key scripture that sustained me:

....

....

- How did this week bring me closer to fulfilling my vision?

....

....

Conclusion

Congratulations on completing the V.I.S.I.O.N.A.R.Y. Workbook! Through this journey, you've not only learned the skills and perspectives that define a visionary but have also actively applied them to transform your approach to achieving your goals. This workbook has been about equipping you to live with intention, creativity, and resilience in every aspect of your journey. In this workbook, you've explored:

Vision Driven – Clarifying and focusing on a purpose that aligns with your highest goals.

Imaginative – Cultivating creativity and allowing space for new ideas to flourish.

Strategic Mindset – Planning with purpose and clarity, aligning your actions with your vision.

Innovative – Embracing change and the power of fresh perspectives.

Originator – Developing an original approach that reflects your unique strengths.

Nonconventional – Breaking out of traditional molds and thinking boldly.

Ambitious – Setting your sights high and committing fully to your aspirations.

Risk Taker – Stepping out of your comfort zone and taking calculated risks for growth.

Yielded to the Process – Trusting in the journey, understanding that every stage serves a purpose.

Reflecting on Your Transformation

Look back on where you began this journey and consider the progress you've made in each area of the V.I.S.I.O.N.A.R.Y. framework. Reflect on the moments of insight, the challenges you embraced, and the changes you've implemented in your thinking and actions. Acknowledge these achievements as part of your commitment to growing into your most visionary self.

Moving Forward with Purpose

The path forward is a continuous journey of learning and adapting. The insights and strategies you've gained here are tools you can revisit, refine, and build upon. As you continue to grow, remember that a visionary mindset is flexible—it evolves with each experience, challenge, and success. Keep pushing forward, guided by your vision and anchored by your commitment to originality, ambition, and resilience.

Final Commitment

Close this journey by writing a final commitment to yourself. Set an intention to uphold the values, strengths, and purpose you've built through this workbook. Include affirmations or specific actions that will support you in continuing your visionary journey. This commitment serves as a foundation, reminding you of the steps you've taken and the path you're dedicated to walking.

May your vision propel you, your imagination inspire you, and your ambitions drive you to create a life of purpose and impact. Every step you take as a visionary shapes your future and those around you—embrace it fully, knowing that you're creating something uniquely yours.

Notes

Notes